Contents

Chapter 1
Let's Begin!

Getting started

Some of you starting this book may already have used computers for years. You'll find this book easy – but work through it carefully and you may be surprised to find out lots of things you didn't know!

If you are a 'first-timer', you will probably need a hand from a friend or teacher from time to time.

In this chapter you will type some text and learn how to correct mistakes. You will also be able to save your work so that you can add to it another day.

To do this you will be using **Microsoft Word,** one of many different **word processing packages.**

 Load **Microsoft Word.** You can do this in one of two ways:

 Either double-click the **Word** icon

Microsoft Word

 Or click **Start** at the bottom left of the screen, then click **Programs,** then click

 Microsoft Word

The opening screen

Your screen will look like this:

Title Bar-
Shows the name of
your document

Main Menu Bar-
Choose options to
print, save etc.

Standard Toolbar-
These icons (buttons)
give you quick ways
to print, save etc.

Tip:
If you are using
Word 2000 you will
not see the Task
pane on the right of
the screen.

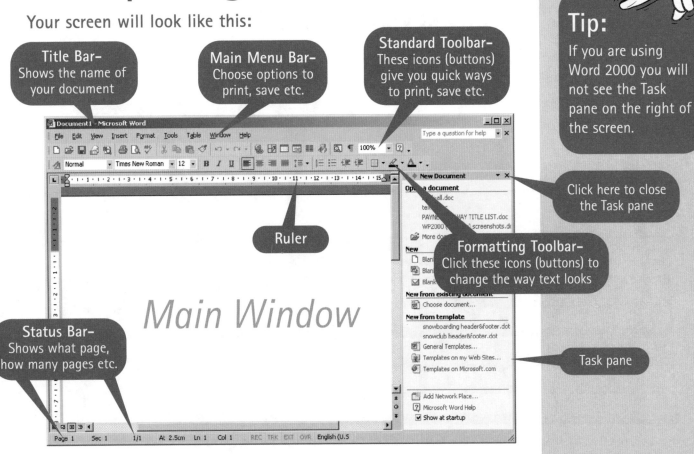

Ruler

Click here to close
the Task pane

Formatting Toolbar-
Click these icons (buttons) to
change the way text looks

Main Window

Status Bar-
Shows what page,
how many pages etc.

Task pane

Figure 1.1: The opening screen

The **Title Bar** shows the name of your document, which might be, for example, a story or letter. If you have not given it a name yet, it will say 'Document1' or perhaps 'Document2' if this is your second story since you started **Microsoft Word** in this chapter.

The **Main Menu** has lots of options for you to choose from. You'll be using it when you need to print or save your story.

The **Standard Toolbar** has a number of **buttons** with little pictures called **icons** which are sometimes clicked instead of choosing from the main menu.

The Formatting Toolbar has icons which let you change the way your text looks – for example, making the letters bigger or smaller.

The area of the screen where you type is called the **main window**.

The **Status Bar** shows what page you are on and how many pages there are in the document – for example 3/6 means you are looking at page 3 of a 6-page document. It also shows a lot of other things which you don't need to know about at this stage.

Note:
The Task pane is
new in Word 2002.
It lists the
documents you
have recently
opened, and other
options. Close it
now by clicking on
the X at the top of
the pane.

The keyboard
Your keyboard will look like this:

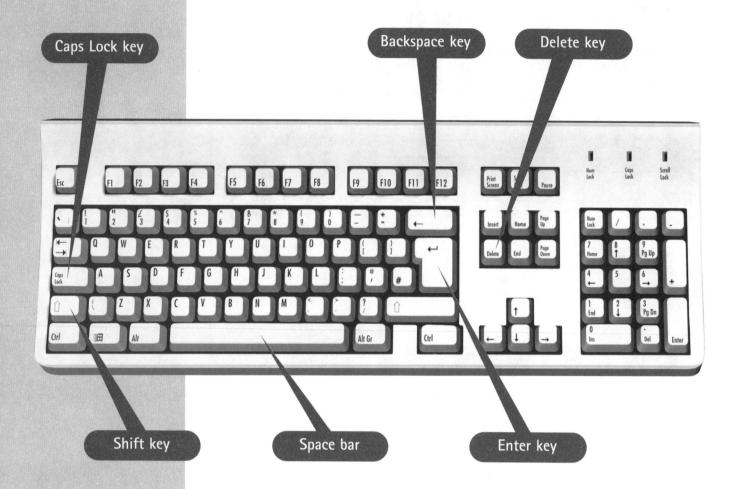

Figure 1.2: The Keyboard

Some of the keys have been labelled on the diagram:

The **Space Bar**.

The **Shift** key. As long as you hold this down, all the letters you type will be in capitals. If a key has 2 symbols, you will type the top one.

The **Caps Lock** key. If you want a whole sentence to be in capitals, you can use the **Caps Lock** key. Just press it once and release it. All the letters you type after that will be capitals. Press **Caps Lock** again when you want to stop typing capitals.

The **Backspace** key. This deletes the letter to the left of where the cursor is flashing. If you are typing something and press a wrong letter, pressing **Backspace** will delete it and you can then type the right letter. Very useful!

The **Delete** key. This deletes the letter to the right of where the cursor is flashing. It is not as useful as the Backspace key for correcting mistakes that you make as you are going along, but you will find it comes in useful.

The **Enter** key. Use this when you want to go to a new line.

There are two **Enter** keys on the keyboard, one marked with a bent arrow and the other marked **'Enter'**. They both do exactly the same thing. People who are typing lists of numbers like to use the one near the numbers, and people who are using the main part of the keyboard to type text use the one near the letters.

Look for the keys mentioned above on your keyboard.

Caps Lock

Delete

Starting to type

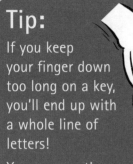

Tip:

If you keep your finger down too long on a key, you'll end up with a whole line of letters!

You can use the **Backspace** key to delete the extra letters!

Type the sentence

My name is Jo.
(or Lucy, Ahmed, or whatever your name is!)

MMMMMMMMMMMMMMMMMMMMMMMMM...

Remember to use the **Shift** key for capital letters.

The pointer, cursor and insertion point

As you move the mouse around, the pointer moves around the screen. The pointer looks different depending on where it is.

When the pointer is in the Ruler it is shaped like an Up arrow pointing left

The flashing cursor marks the insertion point, where the next character will appear when you type

My name is Jo|

When the pointer is in the text area it is shaped like an I-Beam

When the pointer is in the Left Margin it is shaped like an Up arrow pointing right

Figure 1.3: Pointer shapes

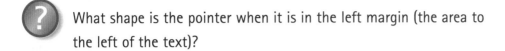 Move the mouse around the screen. How many different shapes does the pointer change into?

What shape is the pointer when it is in the left margin (the area to the left of the text)?

What shape is the pointer when it is in the ruler?

What shape is the pointer when it is in the middle of the screen?

Click in different places in and around your text. The flashing vertical line (cursor) appears in different places.

Position the pointer at the beginning of the line. Make sure that the pointer is the **I-beam** shape, not an arrow shape, before you click.

Type Hello! followed by a space.
Now your text should say
Hello! My name is Jo.

Position the cursor at the end of the line and type What's yours?

Position the cursor just before the **n** of *name* and type first. Now your text should say
Hello! My first name is Jo. What's yours?
(Except that you will have typed your own name, not Jo, of course!)

Where the cursor flashes is called the **insertion point**. That is where text will appear if you start to type.

Spelling

You may see a red wavy line under your name, or under one of the other words in the sentence. This means either you have mis-spelt a word, or that the computer has never heard of your name! (You'll also get a red wavy line if you miss out a space between words, or forget to put a space after a full-stop between sentences.)

▶ Try typing a list of names and see which ones it knows. Press **Enter** after each name and type the next name on a new line.

▶ Insert a new name in the middle of your list.

▶ Experiment with the **Backspace, Delete** and **Enter** keys until you are sure you know what each one does.

▶ If you pressed **Enter** between the two r's in **Darren,** you would end up with

> Alan
> Pat
> **Dar**
> ren
> Sue

Question: How can you put the two halves of **Darren** together again?

Answer: With the insertion point just before **ren,** press **Backspace.**

This deletes the **Enter** character!

Hint:

In the list of names below, if you want to add a new name after **Pat**, you need to click the mouse when the pointer is at the end of **Pat**, to make an **insertion point.**

Then you can press **Enter** to go to a new line and you are ready to type the new name.

Alan

Pat

Darren

Sue

Saving your work

If you want to keep your work so that you can add to it or change it another day, you must keep it safe in a **file** on a disk (this is called **saving a file**).

This could be the hard disk inside the computer, or it could be a floppy disk that you can insert into the floppy disk drive and take out when you have finished saving.

 Click **File** on the main menu, and then click **Save.** You'll see a screen rather like the one below.

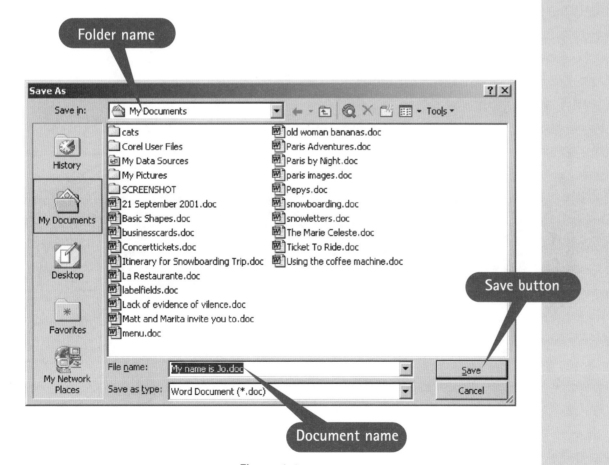

Figure 1.4

Word guesses a name for your file, which will be the first few words you typed. The name appears in the **File name** box.
The file name will be highlighted to show that it is selected ready for you to change it if you want to.
When text is selected you don't have to delete it before typing over it.

 Type a new name. Choose a short name that reminds you what this file is, like Jo1 if your name is Jo.

Microsoft Word will add a full stop and the three letters doc to the name you choose. This shows that it is a document created using **Microsoft Word.**

Your teacher may need to show you in which folder to save your file. In the picture, the document called **My name is Jo** will be saved in a folder called **My Documents.**

 Click the **Save** button. This saves your document and automatically closes the dialogue box.

 Close your document by selecting **File** from the main menu. Then click **Close.**

Chapter 2
Choosing a format

In this chapter you will learn to change the way the text looks by changing the typeface or font. You will also learn to move around the document and use new ways of selecting text so that it can be changed using buttons on the Formatting toolbar.

This **Times New Roman font** is rather dull...

Fonts

So let's change it to Comic Sans MS!!

Font is another word for **typeface.** Both these words describe the actual shape of the letters that appear on the screen when you type. Fonts have different names like **Times New Roman, Arial, Comic Sans MS.**

Look at the Formatting toolbar. The name and size of the **default font** are shown. (Ignore the **Style** box for now.)

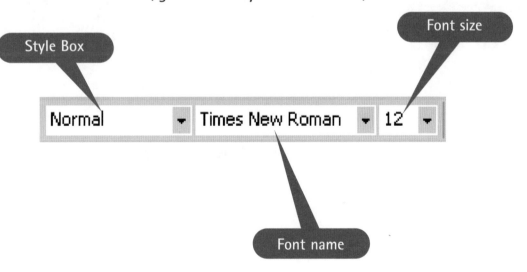

Font size

Style Box

Normal   ▼   Times New Roman   ▼   12   ▼

Font name

Default means what **Microsoft Word** has chosen for you before you change it. So you can have default font name, **default** font size, **default** page size, **default** document name, and so on. Can you think of any other **default** values? (What's the **default** cereal your mother buys unless you ask for something different??)

Project: Design a poster for the school fete.

We're going to use different font styles, sizes and colours to design a poster for a school fete. The finished poster is shown below but don't start typing yet. Follow the instructions in the rest of this chapter!

Note:
Read and follow the instructions for creating this poster, starting on the next page!

School Fete
Saturday 1st July

Bring the whole family!!

Coconut shy
Toss the Welly
Lucky Dip
Pony Rides
Cream Teas

And lots, lots more!!

Lucky Draw Programme 20p

Figure 2.2

Opening a new document

Open a new **Word** document if you don't already have one on your screen. To do this in Word 2002, choose **File, New, Blank Document** as shown below left:

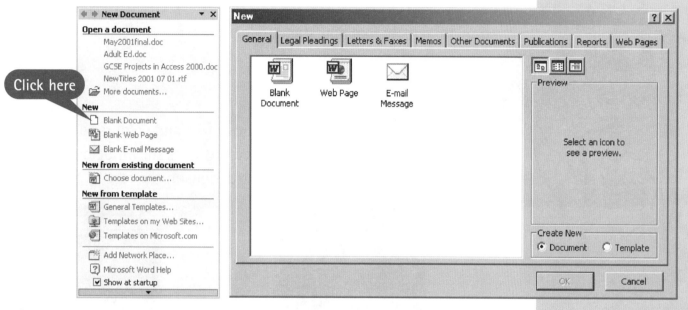

 Click here

Figure 2.3: Opening a new document in Word 2002 (left) and 2000

In Word 2000, choose **File, New** from the main menu. You will see a screen like the one above right. Click **OK**.

Left, right or centre?

When you design a poster you can decide whether you want the text on the left or the right, or if it would look better centred.

You can either type the text first, and then arrange it on the page how you want it, or you can choose the **font style, size, colour** and **alignment** before you start typing.

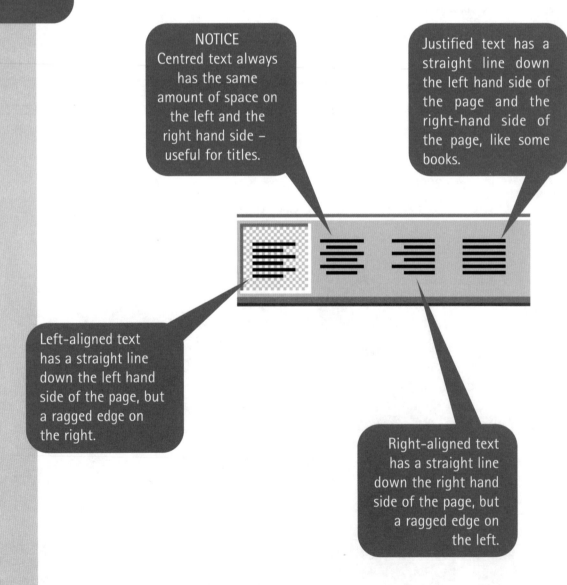

NOTICE
Centred text always has the same amount of space on the left and the right hand side – useful for titles.

Justified text has a straight line down the left hand side of the page and the right-hand side of the page, like some books.

Left-aligned text has a straight line down the left hand side of the page, but a ragged edge on the right.

Right-aligned text has a straight line down the right hand side of the page, but a ragged edge on the left.

Figure 2.4

Let's do it!

 Start by changing the font to **Arial**. To do this, click the down arrow beside the Font name box and a list of fonts will be displayed.

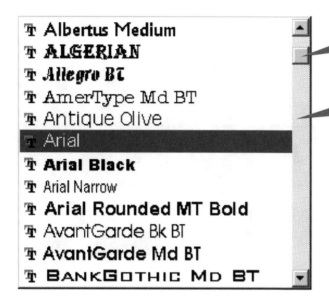

Scroll box

Scroll bar

Figure 2.5

(The list of fonts on your computer may not be the same as the one shown above.)

 Click the arrow by the **Font Size** box. Scroll down the list of sizes and choose a large font size – try 72.

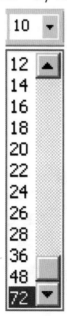

Figure 2.6

Tip:

There are three different ways to scroll down a list or a window.

1. Drag the scroll box downwards (see Figure 2.5).

2. Click in the scroll bar below the scroll box to scroll larger distances.

3. Click the arrow head at the bottom of the scroll bar to scroll one line at a time.

The first three lines of the poster will have the text **centred** – that means not over to the left or the right but in the middle of the page. The text will also be **bold – like this!**

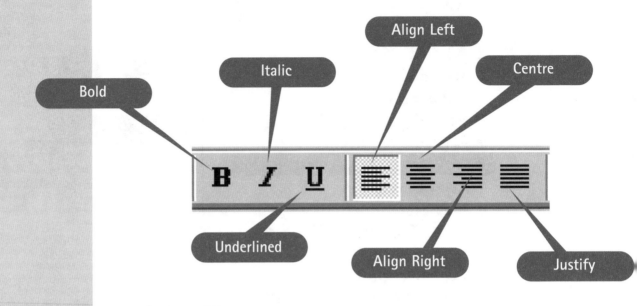

Figure 2.7

Click the **Centre** button and the **Bold** button. They will look pressed in when they are selected – like the **Align Left** button in the picture above.

Type School Fete and then press **Enter.**

Now click the **Bold** button again to de-select it.
It should no longer look as though it's pressed in.

Change the font size to **36.** Type the next line of the poster, Saturday 1st July.

Fee's Tip:

De-select is the opposite of **select.** A button that is selected looks pressed in. Clicking it again de-selects it and restores it to its normal appearance. When text is selected, it is highlighted. When you de-select it by clicking away from it, the highlighting disappears.

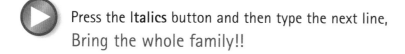 Press **Enter** twice.

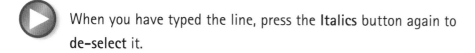 Press the **Italics** button and then type the next line,
Bring the whole family!!

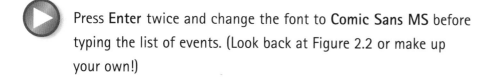 When you have typed the line, press the **Italics** button again to
de-select it.

Press **Enter** twice and change the font to **Comic Sans MS** before
typing the list of events. (Look back at Figure 2.2 or make up
your own!)

Making changes to the text format

Sometimes you want to change a font size or make text bold after
you've typed it. Before you can make changes to existing text, you
must **select** it.

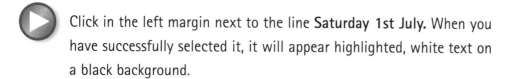 Click in the left margin next to the line **Saturday 1st July.** When you
have successfully selected it, it will appear highlighted, white text on
a black background.

 Choose a different font for this line.

Click away from it to de-select it. The highlighting disappears.

Now that you know how to change the font size and alignment you
can finish off the poster. Experiment with different fonts and sizes!

You can see the whole poster by **zooming out** using the **Zoom** ——————
button at the end of the Standard toolbar. Try selecting 50% or
25%, or you can click in the box and type a value like **40** yourself.
When you press **Enter** the page will appear a different size on
your screen.

 50%

Let's add colour

The last tool on the Formatting toolbar is the one to use for setting the colour of the text. Of course if you don't have a colour printer, it won't show up when you print your poster!

 First select the line(s) of text that you want to colour. Click the arrow next to the font colour button and some coloured squares appear for you to choose from. Click one to choose a colour.

 Colour as many lines as you want to.

Nearly there – save and print!

Before you save and print your poster, it would be a good idea to type your name in small letters somewhere on the poster so you know which is yours when 23 posters come rolling off the printer. Do that now.

 Click **File** on the main menu and then click **Save**. Choose a file name (e.g. **School Fete**) and make sure you are saving in the right folder.

 When your teacher says you can print, click the **Print** button on the standard toolbar.

Click **File** on the main menu and then **Close** to close your document.

Chapter **3**
More About Fonts

Now you're ready to type a longer piece of text and alter its appearance. You'll find it has a lot of spelling mistakes – try and type it just as it is written.

A letter to the newspaper in 1849

The letter below was written to the Times newspaper in 1849 and signed by 54 people living in London. Read it through first. You'll be using it to practise entering and changing text.

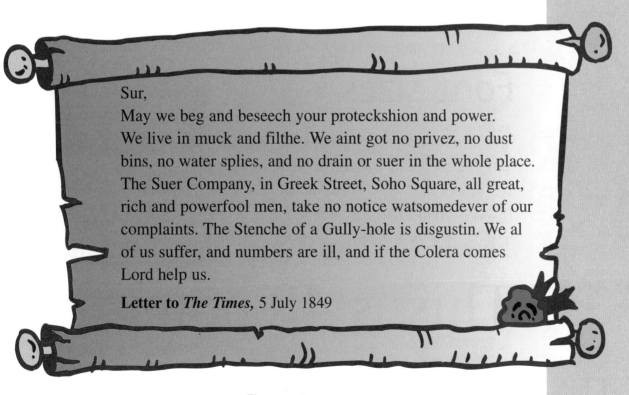

Sur,
May we beg and beseech your proteckshion and power.
We live in muck and filthe. We aint got no privez, no dust
bins, no water splies, and no drain or suer in the whole place.
The Suer Company, in Greek Street, Soho Square, all great,
rich and powerfool men, take no notice watsomedever of our
complaints. The Stenche of a Gully-hole is disgustin. We al
of us suffer, and numbers are ill, and if the Colera comes
Lord help us.

Letter to *The Times,* 5 July 1849

Figure 3.1

Types of font

There are two basic types of font, called **Serif** and **Sans Serif.** A serif is the little tail at the top and bottom of each letter.

This is written in a Serif font called Times New Roman

This is written in a Sans Serif font called Arial

If you know any French you'll realise that **Sans Serif** means literally "without Serif". Sans Serif fonts are very clear and are used on road signs and on the London Underground, for example.

Serif fonts are more often used for large amounts of text that will be read quickly, like newspapers or books. The serifs 'lead your eye' on to the next word.

You should not use too many different fonts on a page – it can end up looking a bit of a mess.

Font sizes

Font sizes are measured in **points.** 6 point is about the smallest font you can read without a magnifying glass.

This is 6 point Times New Roman

This is 12 point Times New Roman

This is 24 point Times New Roman

This is 48 point

 Open a new **Word** document if you don't already have one on your screen. To do this, click the **New Document** button on the toolbar.

Typing the text

▶ Change the **font size** to 14 by clicking the arrow by the Font Size box and selecting **14.**

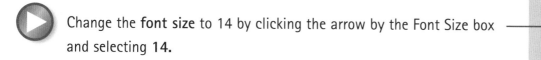

▶ Type the first two or three sentences of the text. Remember to press **Enter** after typing **Sur,** but don't press **Enter** at the end of each line. **Word** will automatically go to a new line when it reaches the end of the line.

Selecting text

When you want to make some changes to some text you have already typed, you have to **select** it first.

When text is selected, it shows up highlighted, white on a black background.

▶ Try these two ways of selecting **Sur** and the first sentence.

First way:

▶ Use the mouse to put the pointer to the left of the first letter (S).

▶ Click the left mouse button to move the **insertion point.** The insertion point is where text will appear when you start typing.

▶ Then hold the left mouse button down while you drag down and across to the end of the first sentence.

▶ Release the button and the text should stay white in a black background.

Sur,

May we beg and beseech your proteckshion and power. We live in muck and filthe We aint got no privez, no dust bins, no water splies, and no drain or suer in the whole place.

Figure 3.2: Selected text

▶ Now click anywhere in the window away from your selected text to de-select it so that you can try out the second way. It should lose its black background (highlighting) and return to normal text.

Second way:

The second way is useful when you want to select whole lines of text.

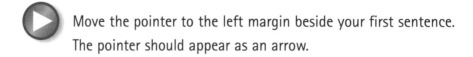 Move the pointer to the left margin beside your first sentence. The pointer should appear as an arrow.

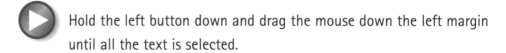 Hold the left button down and drag the mouse down the left margin until all the text is selected.

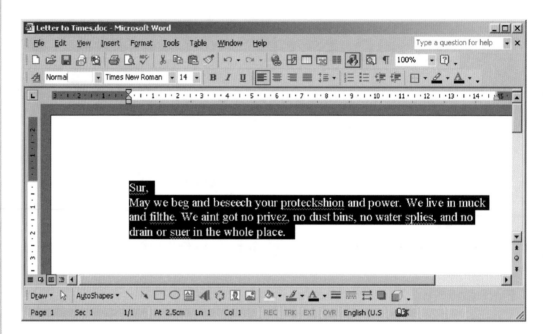

Figure 3.3

Typing and adjusting the rest of the letter

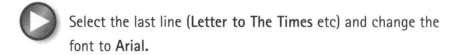 Enter the rest of the letter and the last line.

Select the last line (**Letter to The Times** etc) and change the font to **Arial.**

Select the words **Letter to The Times** and make it bold.

Select **The Times** and make it italic.

Justified text

Text is **justified** when it goes straight down the left and right margins. At the moment, your text should be **left-aligned.** Books and newspapers often use justified text.

 Select the whole of your text.

 Click the **Justify** button on the Formatting toolbar. ——————————

Sur,

May we beg and beseech your proteckshion and power. We live in muck and filthe. We aint got no privez, no dust bins, no water splies, and no drain or suer in the whole place. The Suer Company, in Greek Street, Soho Square, all great, rich and powerfool men, take no notice watsomedever of our complaints. The Stenche of a Gully-hole is disgustin. We al of us suffer, and numbers are ill, and if the Colera comes Lord help us.

Letter to *The Times*, 5 July 1849.

Figure 3.4: Justified text

 Click the mouse at the end of the document after **1849.**
Press **Enter** twice.

 Type your name.

When Emma typed the letter, she made 7 mistakes.

Did you do any better?

Saving and printing your work

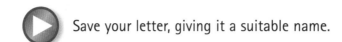

▶ Save your letter, giving it a suitable name.

▶ When your teacher says you can print, click the **Print** button on the Standard toolbar.

▶ Close the file.

24

Chapter 4
Using Graphics

You can add pictures, scanned photographs or cartoons to your documents.

There are a few clip art images stored with **Microsoft Word.** You can also buy CDs with thousands of pictures and graphics of all kinds.

Project: Write a short story or article and illustrate it.

We are going to write a short essay about a frog and use clip art to liven it up. When you have practised the new skills, you can write about something that interests you and find some suitable clip art to import.

 Open a new document by clicking the first icon on the Standard toolbar.

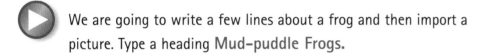 We are going to write a few lines about a frog and then import a picture. Type a heading Mud–puddle Frogs.

 Make the heading **Arial** font, **20 point, Bold** and **Centred.**

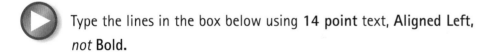 Type the lines in the box below using **14 point** text, **Aligned Left,** *not* **Bold.**

Mud-puddle Frogs

Mud-puddle frogs live in Central America. The male mud-puddle frog sings to attract the attention of the female, and the bigger he is, the louder and lower-pitched he can make his song. Females prefer big strong males and so choose a bass rather than a tenor.

Figure 4.1

 Press **Enter** twice so that you have two blank lines at the end of the document.

Importing clip art

You may have a CD with some clip art you can use. Clip art is simply a collection of pictures and drawings that have been drawn by professional artists and collected together for other people to use. **Microsoft Word** comes with a small collection of clip art.

 Click **Insert** on the main menu. Click **Picture** and then **Clip Art...**

A task pane or window something like one of those below will appear.

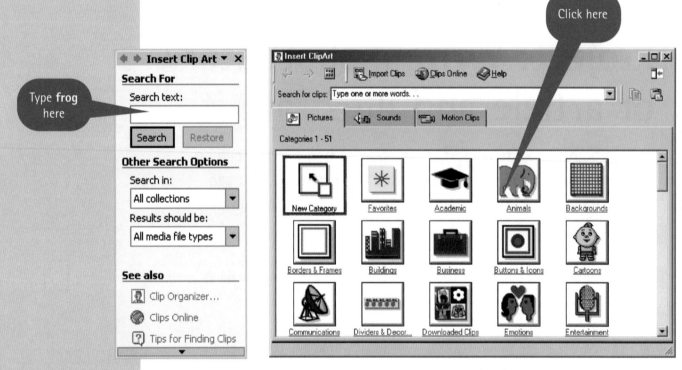

Figure 4.2: Inserting clip art in Word 2002 (left) and 2000

In Word 2002

 Type frog in the search text box and click **Search**. Scroll down the frog pictures to find the one shown below, then click on it.

 Close the **Insert ClipArt** task pane.

In Word 2000

Click the
Insert Clip icon

 Click Animals in the list of categories and a new set of
pictures appears.

 Click the picture of the frog then click the **Insert clip** icon from the
menu that pops up.

The picture of the frog is now inserted into your document.

It's far too big so you need to be able to see more of the page on
your screen.

 Click the arrow beside the **Zoom** button and click 75%. ——— 75% ▾

Now your document should look like the one below:

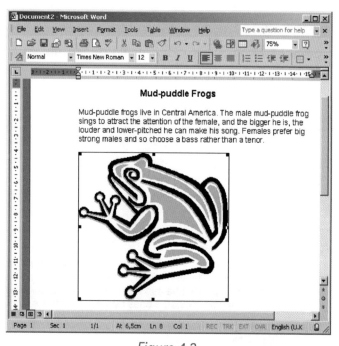

Figure 4.3

 Note the little squares surrounding the graphic (picture).
These are called **handles.** When the handles are visible, the
graphic is **selected.**

 Click away from the graphic and the handles disappear.

Click anywhere inside the graphic and the handles will be
visible again.

Tip:
If you cannot find a
frog picture, you could
make up a story about
a turtle or another
animal instead!

Changing the size of the graphic

You can make the graphic bigger or smaller without changing its proportions by dragging any of the corner handles.

▶ Make sure the graphic is selected so that the handles are visible.

▶ Move the pointer over the bottom right handle until it is shaped like a diagonal two-headed arrow.

▶ Click and hold down the left mouse button. The pointer changes to a cross-hair.

▶ Drag inwards and upwards. A dotted rectangle shows how big the graphic will be when you release the mouse button. When it is about a third the width of the text, release the button.

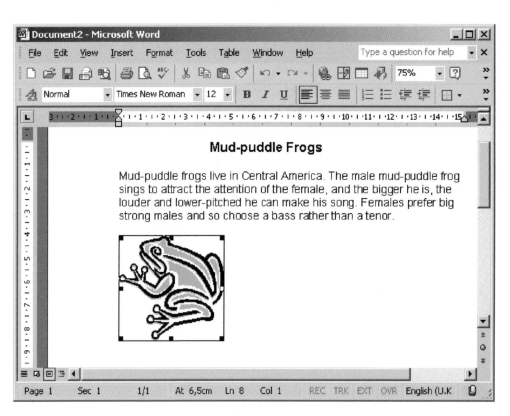

Figure 4.4

Moving a graphic

When the handles are black like this you cannot drag a graphic. It would be more convenient to be able to move it anywhere with the mouse.

 Click the frog with the right hand mouse button. A **shortcut (pop-up) menu** appears.

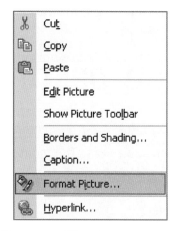

Figure 4.5: The shortcut menu

 Click **Format Picture**, near the bottom of the menu.

 The **Format Picture** window appears. Click the tab labelled **Layout**, as shown below.

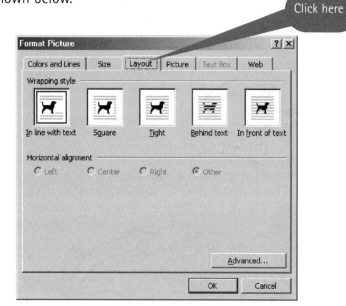

Figure 4.6: The Format Picture window

The **wrapping style** is now **In line with text** which means the graphic is part of the text and can't be moved about.

Tip:
You can only move it using the **Align Left, Centre**, etc tools on the Formatting toolbar.

 Click the **Square** wrapping style, then click **OK**.

Figure 4.7

The frog now has white handles.

 Click in it and you'll find you can drag it about.

Copying and pasting graphics

Suppose you want to have three frogs. Instead of inserting the graphic three times, you can copy and paste.

 Click the frog to select it.

 Click the **Copy** button on the Standard toolbar.

 Click the **Paste** button on the Standard toolbar.

 Click **Paste** again to create a third frog.

 You can move the frogs anywhere you like on the page by dragging them.

Mud-puddle Frogs

Mud-puddle frogs live in Central America. The male mud-puddle frog sings to attract the attention of the female, and the bigger he is, the louder and lower-pitched he can make his song. Females prefer big strong males and so choose a bass rather than a tenor.

Drag here to move the frog

Figure 4.8

Distorting a graphic

Distorting a graphic means changing its shape. This will happen if you drag one of the side handles.

▶ Space out your frogs down the page so that they do not overlap. (To do this, select each one in turn and drag it to a new place, keeping away from the handles.)

▶ Select a frog and drag the middle right handle to the right. It will look as though it is about to jump!

▶ Select another frog and drag the top middle handle upwards.

Your page may look something like the one below now. You may need to make the frogs smaller to fit them all on a line.

Mud-puddle Frogs

Mud-puddle frogs live in Central America. The male mud-puddle frog sings to attract the attention of the female, and the bigger he is, the louder and lower-pitched he can make his song. Females prefer big strong males and so choose a bass rather than a tenor.

Figure 4.9

Placing text around a graphic

When you move your frogs around the page the text may move too. This happens when you move the frog up into the text.

Sometimes you may want to have writing next to a graphic, or around it, or even on top of it.

To practise this, we only need one frog.

 Select one of the distorted frogs, and press the **Delete** key. Repeat for the other one.

 Select the remaining frog and make it about a quarter as wide as the text. Move it around in the text.

Notice the text flows or **wraps** around the square of the graphic.

Mud-puddle Frogs

Mud-puddle frogs live in Central America. The male mud-puddle frog sings to attract the bigger he is, can make his males and so tenor. the attention of the female, and the louder and lower-pitched he song. Females prefer big strong choose a bass rather than a

Figure 4.10

You might want the text to be only on one side.

 Click the frog and move it to the right-hand side.

Mud-puddle Frogs

Mud-puddle frogs live in Central America. The male mud-puddle frog sings to attract the attention of the female, and the bigger he is, the louder and lower-pitched he can make his song. Females prefer big strong males and so choose a bass rather than a tenor.

Figure 4.11

Ordering graphics

 Copy the frog and press the **Paste** button several times to create several frogs.

Mud-puddle Frogs

Mud-puddle frogs live in Central America. The male mud-puddle frog sings to attract the attention of the female, and the bigger he is, the louder and lower-pitched he can make his song. Females prefer big strong males and so choose a bass rather than a tenor.

Figure 4.12

Now you can move the frogs under the text and make some of them smaller.

 Drag the frogs separately under the text.

 Make some of them smaller.

To get the smaller frogs to seem furthest away, they need to be at the back. You can change the order in which they appear.

 Right-click a frog that you want at the back and from the pop-up menu select **Order**.

 Select **Send to Back**.

 You can try bringing other frogs to the front by right-clicking them, selecting **Order** and then **Bring to Front** or **Bring Forward**.

If the frogs jump about when another is moved next to them, just move them back!

Grouping graphics

Sometimes it is useful to group individual graphics into one graphic so that you can move everything together.

 On the Drawing toolbar at the bottom of the screen, click the arrow tool.

 Select all the frogs by dragging right around them with the arrow tool.

 Right-click and select **Grouping**, and then select **Group**.

You will see that just one set of handles replaces the handles around each frog. They can now be moved as a single graphic.

Mud-puddle Frogs

Mud-puddle frogs live in Central America. The male mud-puddle frog sings to attract the attention of the female, and the bigger he is, the louder and lower-pitched he can make his song. Females prefer big strong males and so choose a bass rather than a tenor.

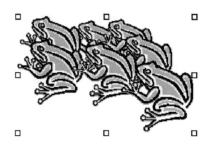

Figure 4.13

Finishing the story

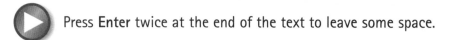 Press **Enter** twice at the end of the text to leave some space.

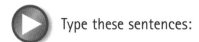 Type these sentences:

Bats, who eat the frogs, listen for the calls and can more easily find the ones with the loudest call. So the male frog has a problem: should he sing loudly and attract a female, or sing quietly and avoid being eaten?

Saving and Printing

 Type your name at the bottom of the story.

 Save your document as **Frogs.**

 To print the story, press the **Print** button on the Standard toolbar.

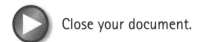 Close your document.

Chapter 5
Longer Documents

In this Chapter you will be creating a longer document, going over more than one page.

Learning to type

Most of us are "two-fingered typists" which means we only use two fingers on the keyboard. (Some of us are three-fingered typists and some people only use one finger, which means you can eat a cheeseburger at the same time but that's not recommended.) Naturally, you are going to be able to type much faster if you learn to type properly without looking at the keyboard. This is called **touch-typing.** This book can't teach you to touch-type, but there are lots of CDs available to help you learn how.

Despite concentrated efforts, Robin failed to master the 'Cheeseburger technique'.

Figure 5.1: The correct rest position for the four fingers of each hand

When you're thinking about what to type next, the fingers of your left hand should rest on **ASDF.** The fingers of your right hand should rest over **JKL;,** with your little finger on the ;. Then you're ready to type with all eight fingers and use your thumbs on the space bar.

On the top row, your little fingers should type the **Q** and the **P**, and on the bottom line, the **Z** and the **/**.

Give it a try!

Writing a story

You are going to type a little bit from each of the first three chapters of 'The BFG' by Roald Dahl.

 Make sure you have a new document open.

 Change the font size to **14.**

 Type the following text.

The Witching Hour
Sophie couldn't sleep.
A brilliant moonbeam was slanting through a gap in the curtains.
It was shining right on to her pillow.
The other children in the dormitory had been asleep for hours.
She slipped out of bed and tip-toed over to the window.
Suddenly she froze. *There was something coming up the street on the opposite side.*
It was something black...
Something tall and black...
Something very tall and very black and very thin.
Who?
It wasn't a human. It couldn't be. It was four times as tall as the tallest human.
Sophie gave a yelp and pulled back from the window. She flew across the dormitory and jumped into bed and hid under the blanket.
And there she crouched, still as a mouse, and tingling all over.
The Snatch
Under the blanket, Sophie waited.

You have typed little extracts from the first three chapters of the book, which have chapter headings **The Witching Hour, Who?** And **The Snatch.**

 Save your file, giving it a suitable name like **BFG.**

 Find the first of these chapter headings, select it by clicking in the margin next to it and make it *Times New Roman*, size **28, Bold** and **Centred.** It will look like this while it is selected:

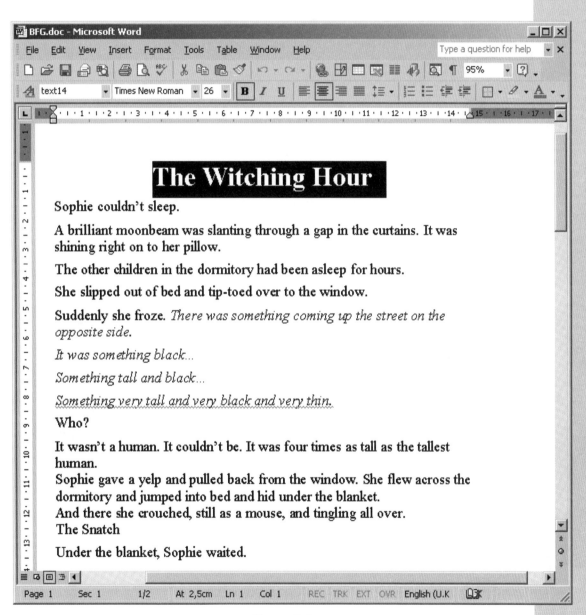

Figure 5.2

The format painter

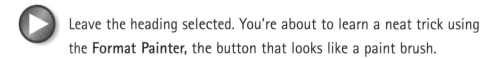

▶ Leave the heading selected. You're about to learn a neat trick using the **Format Painter,** the button that looks like a paint brush.

▶ Double-click the **Format Painter.** Now select the next chapter heading, **Who?** It gets 'painted' with the same format as the original selection.

▶ Now select the third chapter heading, **The Snatch.** That also takes on the same format.

▶ Now click the **Format Painter** once again to turn it off.

Remember if you make a mistake you can undo it with the **Undo** button.

And you can undo the Undo with the **Redo** button!

Tip:

If you click the **Format Painter** once instead of twice (double-clicking) the first piece of text that you select after that will be 'painted' and the Format Painter will then be turned off automatically. Double-click it only when you want to 'paint' several bits of text with the same format.

You need more space between each chapter heading and the first line of the chapter.

▶ Click at the end of the first chapter heading.

▶ Press **Enter.**

▶ Do the same for the other two chapter headings, **Who?** and **The Snatch.**

Starting a new chapter on a new page

We want to start each chapter on a new page. To do that you need to insert a page break just before the second and third chapter headings.

 Click the cursor just before the W of Who?

 From the main menu select **Insert**, then click **Break**.
You'll see a dialogue box appear, like the one shown below.

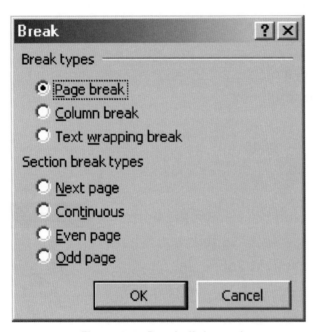

Figure 5.3: Break dialogue box

 Page break is the default selection. Since you want a page break you can click **OK**.

 Now insert another page break just before the third chapter heading, The Snatch.

Hint:

A dialogue box is a little window which is displayed so that you can choose an option or answer a question.

The scroll bars

You can use the **vertical scroll bar** for moving up and down the document.

Up scroll arrow

Scroll up one line
Click the up scroll arrow

Scroll box

Scroll down one line
Click the down scroll arrow

Scroll up one screen
Click above the scroll box

Scroll down one screen
Click below the scroll box

Scroll to a specific page
Drag the scroll box

Down scroll arrow

When you click and hold down the button on the scroll bar, a **tool tip** tells you what page of your document you're on.

(Older versions of Word don't have tool tips though!)

Practise scrolling up and down your document. Sometimes the text seems to disappear completely - probably because you're looking at part of the page that is blank!

Saving a second version of your document

Usually when you save a document a second time, it **overwrites** the original version. That means it just uses the same space again and the original version is lost. Sometimes you may want to keep two different versions.

 Select **File** from the main menu. Click **Save As...**

 Now you can type a new file name, say **BFG2.** You will now have two versions of the story, one with the text before you did any formatting, and the other with each chapter on a new page.

 Close your document.

Chapter **6**
Check that Spelling!

In this chapter you'll be doing some more work on the text you typed in and saved as **BFG2.**

 Open the document containing extracts from 'The BFG'. It should be called **BFG2.**

 Scroll down slowly using the scroll bar without releasing the mouse button until the tool tip tells you that you are on Page 2. Then release the button.

 You're going to add some more text to the end of Chapter 2. Position the cursor just after the full stop at the end of the sentence.

And there she crouched, still as a mouse, and tingling all over.

 Click the mouse so that the cursor is flashing after the full-stop.

 Go to a new line and type the following paragraph. (There are two spelling mistakes in the text below – copy them just as they are.)

Do you know how to get to a new line? Which key should you press – Down Arrow, Right Arrow, Enter or End?

It was so tall its head was higher than the upstairs windows of the houses. Sophie opened her mouth to scream, but no sound came out. Her throte, like her whole body, wos frozen in fright.

It does not matter if you make some spelling mistakes – in fact, you can even make some mistakes on purpose so that you can learn how to correct them!

Your page should look something like this:

Who?

It wasn't a human. It couldn't be. It was four times as tall as the tallest human.

Sophie gave a yelp and pulled back from the window. She flew across the dormitory and jumped into bed and hid under the blanket.

And there she crouched, still as a mouse, and tingling all over. It was so tall its head was higher than the upstairs windows of the houses. Sophie opened her mouth to scream, but no sound came out. Her throte, like her whole body, wos frozen in fright.

Figure 6.1

 Save your file. You can do it the quick way by clicking the **Save** button on the Standard toolbar.

Your file will be saved with the same name it had when you opened it.

It's always a good idea to save your work every few minutes.

One reason is that there could be a power cut or the computer could suddenly 'lock up' for no good reason (that's computers for you). If that happens you will probably have to turn it off and then on again. You will lose all the work you did since you last saved.

Another reason is that if you make some really awful mistakes and can't undo them, you can always close your file without saving it and then open the version you saved before it all went wrong.

Emma remembered to save her work.

Robin didn't, now he's got to start all over again!

Checking the spelling

You'll notice that some words in your text are underlined in red with a wavy line. **Microsoft Word** has a dictionary stored on disk, and the wavy red line usually means that these words are not in its dictionary.

(You'll also get a wavy red line if you type, for example, 'The the tall black figure' because **Word** knows that you didn't really mean to type **'the'** twice.)

If your screen looks like Figure 6.1, you will see two words underlined.

throte

wos

These two words are misspelt.

Correcting individual words

There are several ways you can ask **Word** to check your spelling. You can ask it to check the whole document, or you can just get it to check each word that is underlined in red. That's what we're going to do.

 Put the cursor anywhere in the word **throte** and click the **right hand** mouse button. A little pop-up menu appears:

You are given the following choices:

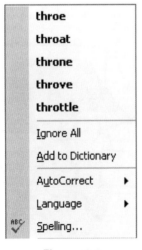

| throe |
| throat |
| throne |
| throve |
| throttle |
| Ignore All |
| Add to Dictionary |
| AutoCorrect ▶ |
| Language ▶ |
| Spelling... |

Figure 6.2

You have to decide which the correct spelling is.

 Click the word once you've decided!

Word will now correct **throte**

 Now right-click the word **wos**.

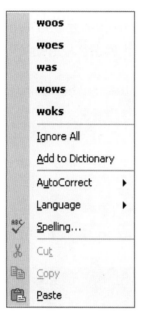

| woos |
| woes |
| was |
| wows |
| woks |
| Ignore All |
| Add to Dictionary |
| AutoCorrect ▶ |
| Language ▶ |
| Spelling... |
| Cut |
| Copy |
| Paste |

Figure 6.3

 Choose the correct spelling.

 Save your file.

Checking the spelling of a whole document

 Open the letter to The Times that you typed and saved in Chapter 3.

This letter has a lot of spelling mistakes in it – it was written by people who did not have the benefits of a word processor and a spelling checker!

 Click the cursor at the very beginning of the document. No text should be selected.

 Click the **Spelling** and **Grammar** button on the Standard toolbar.

A window appears similar to the one below:

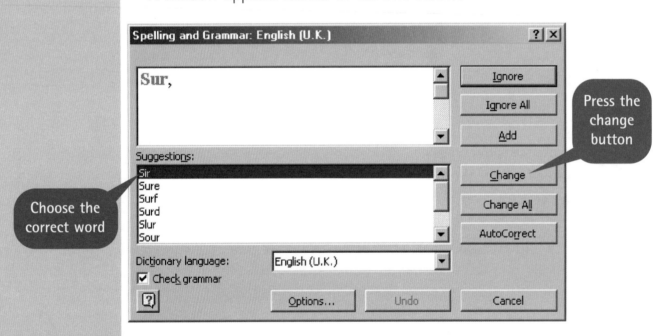

Figure 6.4

 Choose **Sir** from the list of suggestions and click the **Change** button.

The computer automatically moves on to the next word that it does not recognise.

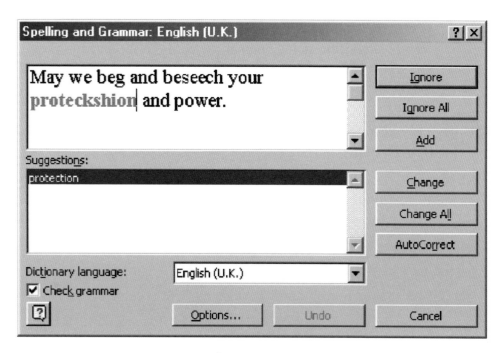

Figure 6.5

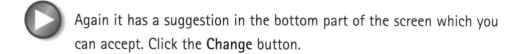 Again it has a suggestion in the bottom part of the screen which you can accept. Click the **Change** button.

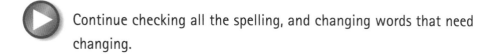 Continue checking all the spelling, and changing words that need changing.

You can leave **aint** unchanged by clicking the **Ignore** button.

When you get to **suer,** Word has a lot of suggestions, all of them wrong!

 Change it to **sewer** in the top part of the screen and click on **Change**.

One word in the letter in Figure 3.4 has not been picked up by **Microsoft Word** even though it is spelt wrong! Can you find it?

You can't rely completely on the spelling checker to find all your mistakes.

If for example you type **widow** instead of **window, Word** would not pick this up. Why?

Save your corrected letter using a different name. It probably doesn't look as interesting as the original one with the spelling mistakes left in!

 Close your document.

Chapter 7
Cutting, Copying and Pasting

Microsoft Word makes it very easy to move text about once you have typed it.

Cutting and pasting

Open the document **BFG2** that you worked on in Chapters 5 and 6.

Use the scroll bar or the **Page Down** key to find the second chapter, entitled **Who?**

Select the text starting **It was so tall..** up to the end of that chapter.

This text is in the wrong place. It needs to be moved to the end of the first paragraph after **tallest human.**

Who?

It wasn't a human. It couldn't be. It was four times as tall as the tallest human.

Sophie gave a yelp and pulled back from the window. She flew across the dormitory and jumped into bed and hid under the blanket.

And there she crouched, still as a mouse, and tingling all over.

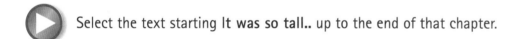
It was so tall its head was higher than the upstairs windows of the houses. Sophie opened her mouth to scream, but no sound came out. Her throat, like her whole body, was frozen in fright.

Figure 7.1

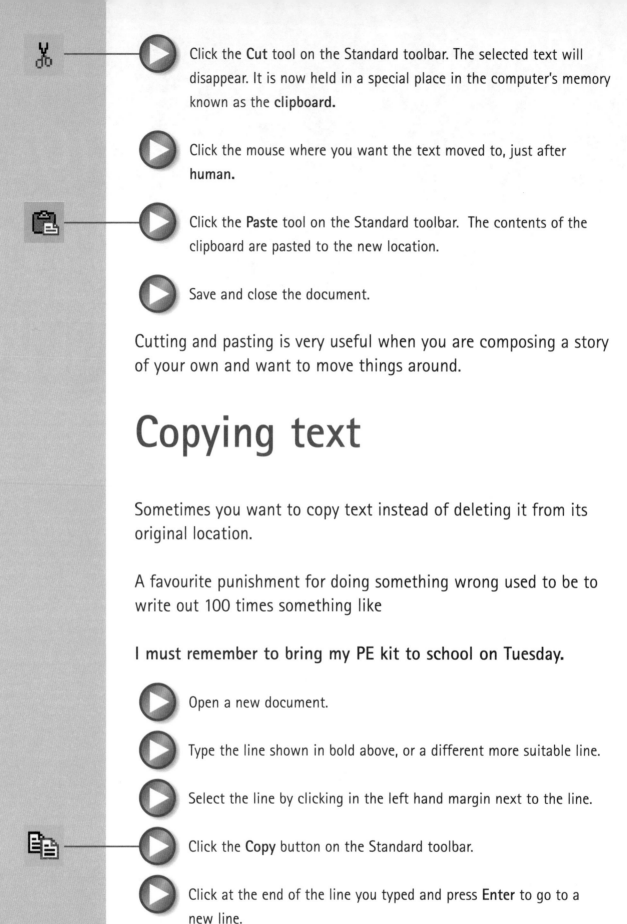

Click the **Cut** tool on the Standard toolbar. The selected text will disappear. It is now held in a special place in the computer's memory known as the **clipboard.**

Click the mouse where you want the text moved to, just after **human.**

Click the **Paste** tool on the Standard toolbar. The contents of the clipboard are pasted to the new location.

Save and close the document.

Cutting and pasting is very useful when you are composing a story of your own and want to move things around.

Copying text

Sometimes you want to copy text instead of deleting it from its original location.

A favourite punishment for doing something wrong used to be to write out 100 times something like

I must remember to bring my PE kit to school on Tuesday.

Open a new document.

Type the line shown in bold above, or a different more suitable line.

Select the line by clicking in the left hand margin next to the line.

Click the **Copy** button on the Standard toolbar.

Click at the end of the line you typed and press **Enter** to go to a new line.

Click the **Paste** button.

Now you can select both lines, copy and paste them so that you have 4 lines.

Select the 4 lines, copy and paste them.

It should not take very long before you have the required 100 lines! Remember that the Status bar at the bottom of the screen will show you what line you are on. This should help you to know how many lines you have done.

Finding and replacing text

Now suppose you have just finished copying and pasting all those lines and you realise it is Thursday you are supposed to bring your PE kit, not Tuesday. You need to find a quick way of replacing Tuesday with Thursday in every line.

 Click at the start of the first line.

 From the main menu select **Edit,** and then select **Replace.**

You will see a dialogue box and you can type the word or phrase that you want to replace, and the word or phrase to replace it with.

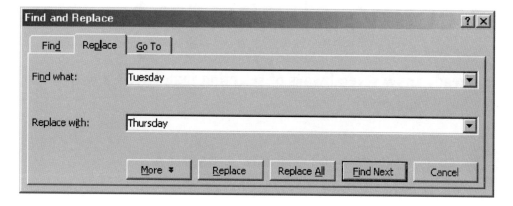

Figure 7.2: Searching for and replacing text

You can get the computer to replace all occurrences, or search for them one at a time so that you can decide whether or not to replace each one. In this case you want them all replaced.

 Press the button marked **Replace All.**

Word tells you how many words have been replaced.

I must remember to bring my PE kit to school on Thursday
I must remember to bring my PE kit to school on Thursday

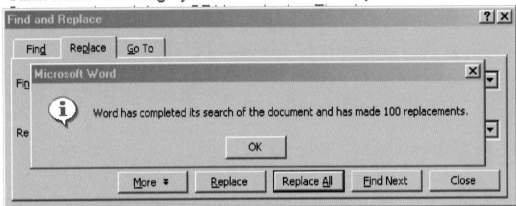

I must remember to bring my PE kit to school on Thursday
I must remember to bring my PE kit to school on Thursday
I must remember to bring my PE kit to school on Thursday

Figure 7.3

Selecting all the text

You already know several ways of selecting text. Here's a way of selecting all the text.

 On the main menu click **Edit.** Then click **Select All.**

 Now that all the text is selected, change the font size to **14.**

 Now change the font. Try **Wingdings!** Your lines will look as though they are in code.

Wingdings is a font that consists of all kinds of funny symbols.

✌ ♌ ♍ ♎ ♏ ♐ ♑ ♒ ♓ ⅇ ⅋

Inserting special symbols

You can insert special symbols into your text by selecting **Insert** from the main menu. Then click **Symbol...**
Here are some of the special symbols you may need one day:

 Insert the symbol "   on a new line in your document.

Chapter 8

Drawing Tools, Bullets and Borders

In Chapter 4 you imported some clip art to brighten up a page. In this chapter you will be drawing your own simple shapes.

The Drawing toolbar

You can display or hide the Drawing toolbar by clicking the **Drawing** button on the Standard toolbar.

  Click the **Drawing** button once and the Drawing toolbar appears at the bottom of the screen. Click it again and it disappears.

This type of button or switch is called a **toggle**. It works just like the cord you pull to turn the light on or off in the bathroom.

 Open a new **Word** document by clicking the **New** icon on the Standard toolbar.

Type a heading at the top of the page:

BASIC SHAPES

 Make sure the Drawing toolbar is displayed at the bottom of your screen.

Drawing simple shapes

Figure 8.1: The Drawing toolbar

Click the **Rectangle** tool on the Drawing toolbar. ——————— □

Move the pointer on to your blank page and it changes to a cross-hair. Wherever you click now will be the top left hand corner of the rectangle.

Hold the left mouse button down while you drag out a rectangle about the size of the one shown in Figure 8.2.

You should see white handles around the rectangle, showing that it is selected. If there are no handles, click anywhere on the border of the rectangle until handles appear. (Ignore the green handle in Word 2002.)

Change the thickness of the line by clicking the **Line Style** tool on the Drawing toolbar.

Select a line thickness, say 1 pt or 2 pt.

Now click the arrow beside the **Fill** tool. Choose a nice bright colour. ———

Save the document, giving it a suitable name.

Tip:
If you see a large rectangle with the words **Create your drawing here**, select **Tools, Options, General** tab and uncheck **Automatically create drawing canvas when inserting AutoShapes.** Click **OK**.

Tip: You can **change the size** of the rectangle by dragging a corner handle.

You can **move** the rectangle by dragging its border, keeping away from the handles. If the rectangle is filled (e.g. coloured blue or red) you can drag anywhere inside the rectangle to move it.

You can **change the shape** of the rectangle by dragging one of the handles in the middle of a side.

Drawing a square

▶ Click the rectangle tool again but this time hold down the **Shift** key while you drag out a shape on the page. Holding down the **Shift** key ensures that the shape will be a perfect square.

▶ Change the line thickness using the **Line Style** tool.

▶ Click the arrow beside the **Fill** tool and fill the square with a different colour.

Basic Shapes

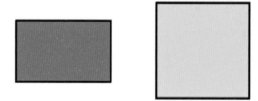

Figure 8.2

Text boxes

Next you can add labels to your shapes by placing a text box under each shape.

▶ Make sure neither of your shapes is selected. (Click away from them if necessary.)

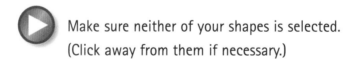 ▶ Click the **Text Box** tool on the Drawing toolbar.

▶ Drag out a box under the rectangle that you have already drawn. (Text boxes are always rectangular.)

▶ Click inside the text box that you have just drawn. An insertion point (vertical line) will flash to show that you can now type text.

▶ Change the font to **Arial, 14 point, Bold, Centred** before you start typing.

▶ Type **Rectangle** (see Figure 8.3).

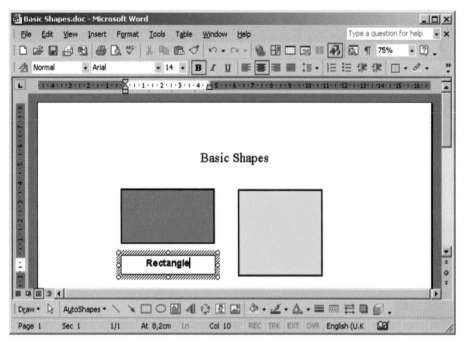

Figure 8.3: Placing a text box

 You can alter the size of the text box if you need to, in the same way as you can alter the size of any graphic. Just drag any of the handles.

When you click away from the text box it may have a black border round it. You probably don't want this.

 Click on the border of the text box to select the box rather than the actual text.

 Click the arrow beside the **Line Color** tool on the Drawing toolbar.

 Select **No Line.**

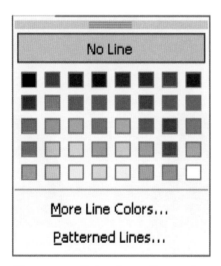

Figure 8.4: Selecting a line colour

 Remember to save your work frequently.

Tip:

You can change the colour of the text in a text box by selecting the box, then clicking the arrow by the **Font Color** tool

A ▾

on the Drawing toolbar.

Placing other shapes

Now place an oval shape. Colour it the same way that you coloured the other shapes.

Place a text box underneath it and type **Oval** in the text box.

Place a circle by holding down the **Shift** key while you place the oval shape.

Colour the circle.

Label it **Circle** using a text box like the one shown in *Figure 8.3*.

3D shapes

You can turn a square into a cube or a circle into a cylinder.

Click the **Rectangle** tool on the Drawing toolbar. Place a square on the page by holding down the **Shift** key while you drag out a rectangle.

With the square selected, click the **3-D** tool at the right hand end of the Drawing toolbar.

Choose one of the shapes. The first one has been chosen in Figure 8.5.

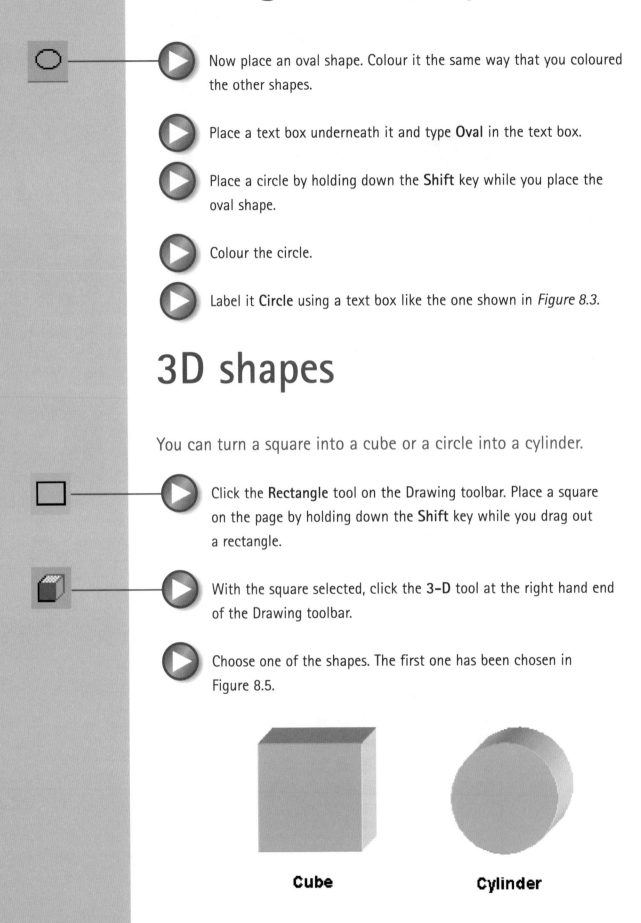

Cube　　　　　　**Cylinder**

Figure 8.5: 3-D shapes

Colour and label your cube using a text box as before.

 Now create and label a cylinder in a similar way.

Have a look at **Autoshapes** on the Drawing toolbar.
You can place other shapes,
colour them and label them.

Having chosen the **Heart Autoshape**, *Robin suffered the embarrassment of displaying his work to the whole class!*

Finishing touches

Use the **Zoom** button to change the view of your page to ——————— 50% so that you can see most of the page on the screen.

Drag the shapes and text boxes around until you are satisfied with their arrangement on the page. Be sure everything fits on one page.

 Save your work.

Print out the document when you have permission to do so.

 Close your document.

Fee's Tip:
You can select a shape and its text box and then move them together. Click the shape, then hold down the **Shift** key while you click the text box. For moving small distances, use the arrow keys.

Bullets and Borders

Finally you'll create a poster to display in the classroom to tell pupils what to do in case of fire.

Fire Alarm Procedures

- In case of fire inform any member of staff.
- Leave the building in silence by the nearest exit.
- Take nothing with you.
- Line up at the Fire Assembly point.
- When the register is called, just say 'Yes'.
- Do not go back into the building until the Fire Officer gives permission.

Figure 8.6

 Open a new document.

 Select a suitable font for the title. The one in the figure is **Albertus Extra Bold**, size **36** points.

 Type the heading.

 Change to a different font. The one in the figure is **Albertus Medium, 24** point.

Making bullets

▶ Click the **Bullets** tool on the Formatting toolbar. ⎯⎯⎯⎯⎯⎯⎯⎯⎯⎯⎯⎯

▶ Type the instructions. Each time you press **Enter,** a bullet will automatically appear on the next line.

▶ After you have typed the last item in the list, press **Enter** once more.

▶ Turn off the bullets by clicking the **Bullets** tool again.

▶ Select the list by dragging across each bullet point. (Or drag down the left hand margin.)

▶ Click the **Numbering** tool. Your list should now have numbers instead of bullets.

▶ Now click the **Bullets** tool again to change back to bullets instead of numbers.

Spacing out the paragraphs

Every time you press **Enter,** you create a new paragraph.
In your list, **Microsoft Word** treats each bullet point as a separate paragraph. You can put extra space between each bullet point so that the list neatly fills the page.

▶ If the list is not already selected, select it now.

▶ Click the right hand mouse button to display a shortcut menu.

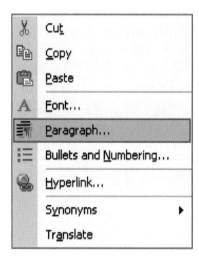

Figure 8.7

Select **Paragraph...** The following window appears:

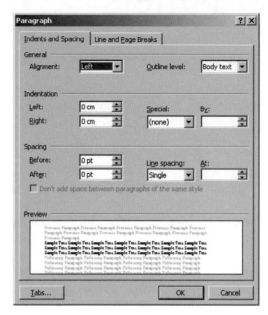

Figure 8.8

In the **Spacing Before** box, click the Up arrow until **12** is displayed.

Click **OK.**

If that is not enough spacing, try again. You can increase the **Spacing Before** to 18, or you could insert some **spacing after** each paragraph using the **Spacing After** box.

Keep experimenting until you are satisfied with the layout.

Putting a border round the list

You can put a border round the list and its heading.

Click anywhere in the text.

On the main menu click **Edit.** Then click **Select All.**

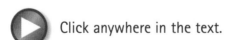 Click the **Outside Border** button on the Formatting toolbar.

Shading the title

▶ Select the title by clicking in the left margin next to it.

▶ On the main menu, select **Format.** Then click **Borders and Shading...**

▶ A dialogue box will appear:

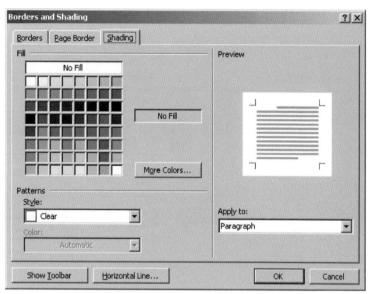

Figure 8.9

▶ Make sure the **Shading** tab is selected.

▶ Choose a shade.

▶ Click **OK.**

▶ When you are happy with your document, save and print it.
Finally, here's a quick way to close your document.

▶ Click the **Close** icon in the top right hand corner of your screen. ────

That's the end of this introduction to word processing. You are already more expert than about 90% of **everyone** over 30 in this country!

Index